ire

Compiled by Terry Marsh

JARROLD
publishing

Mapping
sourced from
Ordnance
Survey®

Text: Terry Marsh
Photography: Terry Marsh
Editor: Crawford Gillan
Designer: Ellen Moorcraft

OS Ordnance Survey This product includes mapping data licensed from Ordnance Survey® with the permission of the Controller of Her Majesty's Stationery Office. © Crown Copyright 2002. All rights reserved. Licence number 100017593. Ordnance Survey, the OS symbol and Pathfinder are registered trademarks and Explorer, Landranger and Outdoor Leisure are trademarks of the Ordnance Survey, the national mapping agency of Great Britain.

Jarrold Publishing ISBN 0-7117-2430-X

While every care has been taken to ensure the accuracy of the route directions, the publishers cannot accept responsibility for errors or omissions, or for changes in details given. The countryside is not static: hedges and fences can be removed, field boundaries can alter, footpaths can be rerouted and changes in ownership can result in the closure or diversion of some concessionary paths. Also, paths that are easy and pleasant for walking in fine conditions may become slippery, muddy and difficult in wet weather, while stepping-stones across rivers and streams may become impassable.

If you find an inaccuracy in either the text or maps, please write or e-mail to Jarrold Publishing at one of the addresses below.

First published 2003
by Jarrold Publishing

Printed in Belgium
by Proost NV, Turnhout. 1/03

Jarrold Publishing
Pathfinder Guides, Whitefriars,

ld.com
co.uk

'alace
d and poppies,

Contents

Keymap

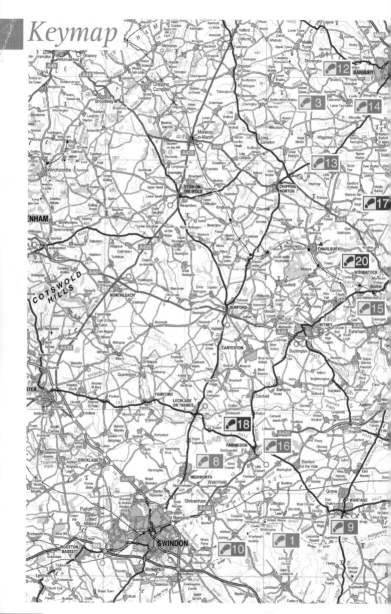

SCALE 1:454 545 or 1 INCH to about 7 MILES *1CM to 4.4KM*

KEYMAP HEIGHTS SHOWN IN FEET

Introduction

The routes and information in this book have been devised specifically with families and children in mind. All the walks include points of interest and a question to provide an objective.

If you, or your children, have not walked before, choose from the shorter walks for your first outings, although none of the walks is especially demanding. The purpose is not simply to get from A to B, but to enjoy an exploration, which may be just a steady stroll in the countryside, alongside rivers and lakes, or through woodlands.

The walks are graded by length and difficulty, but few landscapes are truly flat, so even short walks may involve some ascent, although this is nowhere excessive. Details are given under Route Features in the first information box for each route. The precise nature of the ground underfoot, however, will depend on recent weather conditions. If you do set out on a walk and discover the going is harder than you expected, or the weather has deteriorated, do not be afraid to turn back. The route will always be there another day, when you are fitter or the children are more experienced or the weather is better. Few of the walks in this book involve rough terrain (although there are a number of steep grassy slopes and some muddy going after rain), but it is always advisable to wear proper walking footwear rather than trainers or wellington boots.

Bear in mind that the countryside is constantly changing. Landmarks may disappear, gates may becomes stiles, rights-of-way may be altered, permissive paths may close. In quite a few places the terrain can be confusing, and this means having to pay rather close attention to route descriptions and waymarking or, in the absence of waymarking, the general direction followed by the path. But none of the walks is so complex as to deter anyone.

Village Hall, Buscot

Some of the paths are seasonally overgrown. This presents two problems: one is difficulty in following the route underfoot; the other is the soaking you may get from overgrowth if you do the walk after rain, or stinging by nettles, which will be a problem for young children and also makes the wearing of shorts something to be wary of. Arable fields, while invariably having a wide field header to walk along, often have crops that spread or are blown down by the wind, and this obscures the 'kerb' between the field margin and the crop, producing the risk of ankle sprain.

Oxfordshire

Beyond the university bustle and architectural wealth of Oxford, an ancient settlement described by poet Matthew Arnold as 'that sweet City with her dreaming spires', Oxfordshire bridges the gap between the Thames valley and the Midlands, the Chilterns and the Cotswolds, and is rich in history, folklore, modern enterprise and stately buildings.

The county undoubtedly grew in stature when, in a re-organisation of local government boundaries in 1974, it acquired the Vale of White Horse from Berkshire, with it bringing a remarkable concentration of prehistoric wonders set along an ancient trade route.

In a compact area south of the village of Uffington, the White Horse, is Britain's oldest hillside carving. The scouring of the horse was a customary duty of nearby villages in the Hundred of Hildeslow, which in later years became an occasion for fairs and games. A short walk from the White Horse stands Uffington Castle, a huge Iron Age hillfort, of which only grass-covered ramparts remain. Its proximity to the White Horse and its position astride the prehistoric trade route known as the Ridgeway, which runs from the coast near Dover to Ilchester in Somerset, lend weight to the suggestion that this may have marked the boundary between two Iron Age tribes.

A mile's easy walking west along the Ridgeway is a large neolithic burial mound, concealed in a woodland glade, and known since before the Norman Conquest as Wayland's Smithy. A Saxon charter of 955 AD names the site 'Welandes Smidthan'. Welande, or Wayland, was a mythical blacksmith, the son of a sailor hero and a mermaid, who married a Valkyrie and went to live with the immortals, making armour for the gods. The legend of Wayland's Smithy decrees that if a traveller's horse loses a shoe, he had only to bring it to this place and leave the horse and some money. Upon his return, the money would be gone and the horse shod.

Oxfordshire is rich in small towns and villages, distinctive ironstone communities preserved in aspic, like Great Tew, a clutch of thatched, box-hedged, honey-coloured cottages that soak up the sun, and a 17th-century, ivy-clad pub. Dorchester, graced by the abbey of St Peter and St Paul, was once a capital of England and a Roman garrison town. It was here that the pagan King of Wessex was baptised by Birinus, the Pope's missionary, a significant event, that began the spread of Christianity throughout southern England, and admitted the head of the royal house, from which our royal family traces its descent, to the Christian faith. Nearby Little Wittenham and Days Lock are the annual venue for a Poohsticks Championship, the sort of idiosyncratic eccentricity in which Britain is distinguished.

Rasham Eyecatcher, Steeple Aston

The appeal of Stoke Row is less instantly noticeable. Once an important centre for the clay industries, the village, set in dry heathland, used to be notoriously short of water. So, the villagers must have been hugely grateful when, in 1863, the Maharajah of Benares gave them their first well, an oriental canopied dome supported on cast-iron columns, as a token of his gratitude for work carried out in India by Edward Anderson Reade of nearby Ipsden.

Each town in Oxfordshire is uniquely distinctive and there is great individuality. Banbury has its Cross, Burford and Bloxham their magnificent churches, Henley is dominated by the Thames and the rowing regatta, Letcombe Bassett, on the edge of the Lambourne Downs, boasts Arabella's Cottage, so named after the character in Thomas Hardy's novel *Jude the Obscure*.

But agriculture has always been important to Oxfordshire, and some idea of its worth can be assessed by the size of the ancient tithe-barns at Great Coxwell (a 13th-century monastic barn) and Swalcliffe (the finest 15th-century half-cruck barn in England).

The county is littered with stately homes, although none rivals the splendour of Blenheim Palace, home of the dukes of Marlborough. Broughton Castle, the home of Lord and Lady Saye and Sele, is magnificent, and a setting for numerous film and television screenplays.

The main attraction of the quiet, farming community of Kelmscott, located on the western boundary of the county, near Faringdon, is the unpretentious manor house dating from 1570. Totally unspoilt and unaltered, and in complete contrast to the Victoriana of his day, Kelmscott was used by arts and crafts disciple William Morris as his country home for the last twenty-five years of his life, its 'Old English' gardens greatly inspiring many of his designs.

Matthew Arnold also described Oxford as a 'Beautiful city…whispering from her towers the last enchantments of the Middle Age.' But walkers exploring this ancient realm will discover for themselves that there is far more to Oxfordshire than the dreaming spires and academia of Oxford.

1 Uffington Castle and the White Horse

START Uffington

DISTANCE 1½ miles (2.6km)

TIME 1 hour

PARKING Woolstone Hill (National Trust)

ROUTE FEATURES Field paths, tracks, narrow lane

This short walk to Uffington Castle and the famous White Horse is steeped in history and, in spite of the crowds that visit it at holiday times, exudes a tremendous sense of peace. There is no doubt that here you are walking through history, which is simply quite wonderful.

Leave the car park at the far left-hand corner by going up a flight of steps to a couple of gates next to a fenced picnic area. The gates give into a large open pasture, and you should turn right

The White Horse, Uffington

PUBLIC TRANSPORT Buses along B4507

REFRESHMENTS Pubs at Woolstone and Uffington

PICNIC AREA Near start

PUBLIC TOILETS None on route

ORDNANCE SURVEY MAPS Explorer 170 (Abingdon, Wantage & Vale of White Horse), Landranger 174 (Newbury, Wantage and surrounding area)

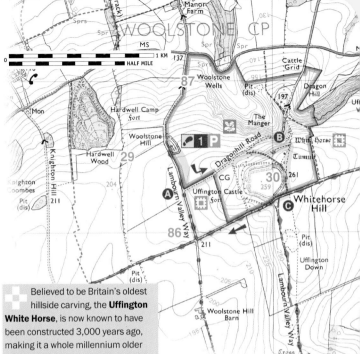

Believed to be Britain's oldest hillside carving, the **Uffington White Horse**, is now known to have been constructed 3,000 years ago, making it a whole millennium older than previously thought. The horse faces north-west, from the top of a steep escarpment on the Berkshire Downs (albeit now in Oxfordshire), measures 374 feet (114m) in length and 110 feet (33m) in height, and is made up of trenches filled with chalk that are up to 10 feet (3m) in width and 2 to 3 feet (1m) deep.

The horse, facing right, is distinctive in its features, a long, disjointed figure, little more than deft brushstrokes on a green canvas, leading to speculation that it is a representation of the mythical dragon slain by St George on nearby flat-topped Dragon Hill – a bare patch of chalk on the summit of the hill is said to be the spot where the dragon's blood was spilled, and upon which no grass will grow.

along a green track, signposted to Wayland's Smithy, which will lead you to a gate giving onto a narrow, surfaced lane.

A Turn left along the lane and follow it to a small car park, just after which, abandon the lane in favour of the lower of two grassy tracks crossing the hillside below the hillfort. This leads shortly to the famous chalk figure, although working out which bit is which at ground level is not easy.

From the White Horse **B** bear right on a gently rising grassy path

Uffington Castle, Hillfort

that leads to the trig pillar marking the summit of Whitehorse Hill. Take time to explore the hillfort, and then return to the trig pillar.

The hillfort is known as **Uffington Castle**. It dates from the Iron Age but only the encircling earth ramparts remain. Its proximity to the **White Horse** and its position astride the prehistoric trade route known as the **Ridgeway** lend weight to the suggestion that this may have been the boundary between two Iron Age tribes, the Dobunni, who were concentrated around Cirencester, and the Atrebates, whose capital was at Silchester.

From the trig pillar, walk towards a gate giving onto the Ridgeway Path **C**, and turn right, following the path, a broad chalk track, down to a track junction. There, turn right (signposted for Woolstone) onto an adjacent track that leads shortly to a surfaced lane. Here, briefly step right to the gate used on the onward section, and through this return across the open pasture to the start of the walk at the Woolstone Hill car park.

? *See if you can find the numbers 2987.*

Castle Hill and Little Wittenham Wood

START Wittenham Clumps
DISTANCE 2 miles (3.4k)
TIME 1 hour
PARKING Wittenham Clumps
ROUTE FEATURES Woodland trails, meadows

2

This gentle walk around the Little Wittenham Nature Reserve and down to the Thames is delightful and full of interest. The diverse range of habitats make the area ideal for wildlife.

Leave the car park by turning through gates and then taking the second path from the right, a grassy track climbing onto Castle Hill.

Pass through the ditch and earthworks of the hill and take a waymarked path into woodland.

Common Mallow

Castle Hill is an Iron Age hillfort with a defensive ditch and earthworks that would have been topped by a timber palisade. Although there have been no major excavations here, ploughing has thrown up pottery over a wide area, showing that the fort was the nucleus of a sizeable settlement.

Walk through the woodland, emerging near a branchless tree on the right. A few more strides leads to a stone monument.

From the monument, set off downhill along a broad, grassy

PUBLIC TRANSPORT Dorchester
REFRESHMENTS Dorchester
PUBLIC TOILETS None on route
ORDNANCE SURVEY MAPS Explorer 170 (Abingdon, Wantage & Vale of White Horse), Landranger 164 (Oxford and surrounding area)

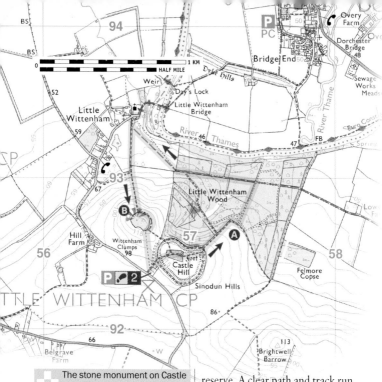

The stone monument on Castle Hill explains that nearby is the **Poem Tree**, so-called because, although now indistinct, a lengthy poem was carved into its bark in the 1840s by Joseph Tubb of nearby Warborough Green.

track with Dorchester abbey church in view in the distance. The track leads down through the defensive ditch and soon emerges to run along a field edge.

Ignore a branching path on the left, but at the next waymark **A**, leave the field edge path and turn into the woodland, which is a nature

reserve. A clear path and track run down through the wood to meet a bridleway just after a wooden barrier.

Turn left along the bridleway, and eventually leave the woodland at a gate.

Take the middle one of three paths, which leads across Church Meadow where, in spring, clumps

> **Can you discover who was ruthless around Castle Hill?**

Little Wittenham from Castle Hill

of Loddon lilies appear, favouring the wet meadows bordering the Thames.

The path leads to the hamlet of Little Wittenham, where the

In Little Wittenham Nature Reserve

church is an attractive place to visit.

Return to Church Meadow and now walk up the right-hand edge of it and then climb on a broad grassy track to reach the edge of Round Hill **B** which provides spectacular views of Oxfordshire, the Cotswolds, the Chiltern Hills and the Ridgeway.

Walk left around the edge of Round Hill (fenced to protect new plantings), and then strike downhill to return to the car park●

3 *Swalcliffe*

START	Swalcliffe
DISTANCE	2¼ miles (3.6km)
TIME	1 hour
PARKING	Village hall or tithe-barn
ROUTE FEATURES	Farmland, Roman road, tracks, roads

This brief walk from the village of Swalcliffe embraces a lengthy period of history from present times back to pre-Roman. The tithe-barn is the most renowned feature here, but the church and the fort on Madmarston Hill all lend intrigue to the region.

Begin from the village hall and walk up the road passing the Church of St Peter and St Paul and then the tithe-barn.

With nine of the original half-crucks and other major roof timbers still intact, **Swalcliffe Barn**, constructed between 1401 and 1407, is the finest half-cruck barn in England, and largely unchanged in 600 years. Known locally as the Tythe Barn, its impressive nature owes much to New College Oxford and William of Wykham, who founded the college in 1379 and endowed it with numerous benefices, including that of Swalcliffe. After restoration by English Heritage in the 1990s, the building was leased to Oxfordshire Museums Services as display storage for local agricultural and trade vehicles.

Continue about another 100 yards (91m) beyond the barn, taking care against approaching traffic, and leave the road by turning onto a signposted bridleway for Epwell on the right **Ⓐ**.

Initially, the bridleway climbs through undergrowth, but then starts to descend into open farmland, as it goes down the right-hand edge of a field. At the bottom of the field, cross a broad track and continue on a signposted route diagonally left across the next field.

The field path leads to a footbridge. Just after the bridge, at a crosspath **Ⓑ**, turn right, shortly cross a stream and then amble

PUBLIC TRANSPORT Buses to Swalcliffe
REFRESHMENTS Pub in Swalcliffe
PUBLIC TOILETS None on route
ORDNANCE SURVEY MAPS Explorer 191 (Banbury, Bicester & Chipping Norton), Landranger 151 (Stratford-upon-Avon, Warwick & Banbury)

Swalcliffe Barn

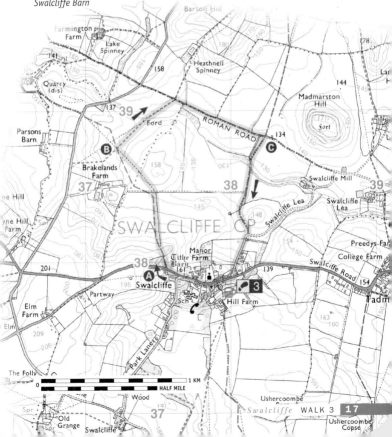

Madmarston Hill (hillfort), Swalcliffe

gently up to meet another broad track, a Roman road flanked on the left by a substantial hedgerow.

Turn right, and when the hedgerow changes direction, go forward across open farmland, now with the grassy mound of Madmarston Hill ahead.

Just after a metal gate, near Madmarston Hill, turn right on a branching track (signposted for Swalcliffe) **C**, and, later, when this swings right, leave it on the apex of the bend by keeping forward along another, less distinct, track leading on to meet a narrow lane.

Turn right and follow the lane up to Swalcliffe village hall and the end of the walk.

There are traces of a Roman settlement near **Madmarston Hill** and an extensive Iron Age hillfort on its summit. Excavations in the fort showed strong evidence of occupation between the first century BC and the first century AD.

The hedgerows and farmlands of North Oxfordshire are bright during spring and summer with wild flowers. See how many different species you can find.

Dorchester and the Thames

The area around Dorchester is steeped in history and is a lovely backdrop to this short walk through the town and across to the River Thames.

START Dorchester

DISTANCE 2½ miles (4.2km)

TIME 1½ hours

PARKING Dorchester (Bridge End)

ROUTE FEATURES Field paths, riverside paths

🥾 Leave the car park at Bridge End and walk into Dorchester, crossing the road to go into the grounds of the Abbey Church of St

The Jesse window, Dorchester Abbey church

Peter and St Paul. A visit to the church is a must as it contains one of the finest examples of a window depicting the Tree of Jesse.

Dorchester became the centre of Christianity in Britain when Bishop Birinus founded a cathedral here in 635. Today, its lovely High Street is flanked by timber-framed cottages, pubs and thatched cottages. The Abbey Church has a curious air about it, but contains some lovely stained glass windows and the rightly famous Jesse window portraying the descent of Christ.

Continue through the main street in Dorchester, walking as far as the memorial at Watling Lane. Turn sharp left along Watling Lane. As the road bends left, leave it for a

PUBLIC TRANSPORT Buses to Dorchester

REFRESHMENTS Pubs in Dorchester

PUBLIC TOILETS At start

ORDNANCE SURVEY MAPS Explorer 170 (Abingdon, Wantage & Vale of White Horse), Landranger 164 (Oxford and surrounding area)

signposted footpath **Ⓐ** branching right for Days Lock.

The path begins between house gardens, but soon breaks out to run along the edge of an arable field. Across the field, the path ends at Dyke Hills.

Common poppy

Dyke Hills is an ancient Iron Age earthwork defining an oppidum (an organised settlement usually found on ancient trade routes rather than a defensive site) forming a roughly rectangular promontory, flanked on two sides by the River Thames and on the other by the River Thame. It may be that this is the site of a settlement that pre-dates the Roman town.

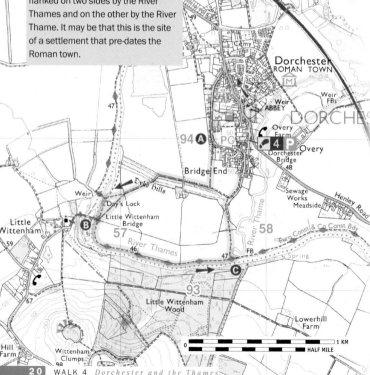

On reaching Dyke Hills, turn right on a broad path and maintain the same direction to a gate giving into a large pasture across which lies Days Lock and the River Thames.

From the gate, take either path – one, on the left, clear, the other less so – leading across to Days Lock. Do not go into the lock complex, but turn left alongside it, walking towards a footbridge **B**.

Do not cross the footbridge, but go beneath it, onto a Thames-side

Days Lock is the site of the **Annual World Poohsticks Championships**. Addicts of *Winnie the Pooh* gather here usually on the first Sunday in January to drop coloured sticks from the bridge.

The Thames, near Dorchester

The Monastery Guest House at Dorchester, built around 1400, is now used as a museum, but has also seen another kind of service. Can you discover what this was?

path. Follow the Thames as far as the inflowing River Thame **C**, and here leave the main river for a field path heading back towards Dorchester.

The path leads on beyond a kissing-gate, and at a second meets a broad path at the edge of an arable field. Turn right, following the path to Bridge End where it meets a surfaced lane and goes past the Catholic Parish Church of St Birinus to return to the start. ●

5 *Stoke Row*

START	Stoke Row
DISTANCE	2¾ miles (4.4km)
TIME	1½ hours
PARKING	Village Hall
ROUTE FEATURES	Woodland, paddocks, stiles, roads

An important centre for the brick-making industry, the village of Stoke Row always had a water supply problem. The villagers must have been relieved, therefore, when, in 1863, the Maharajah of Benares gave them their first well as a token of his gratitude for work carried out in India by Edward Anderson Reade of nearby Ipsden.

Begin the route from the village hall and turn left, crossing the road to visit the Maharajah's Well (or you may prefer to do so on your return).

Looking like an outpost of India and not at all what you might expect in leafy Oxfordshire, the **Maharaja's Well** has an oriental canopied dome supported on cast-iron columns. With a diameter of only four feet, it had to be dug an incredible 368 feet (110m) before striking water, more than twice the height of Nelson's Column in London.

Go past the well, and, near the church, turn left into School Lane. When the lane ends at a farm track, go past the turning to Woodside Farm and then immediately right on a signposted path over a step-stile **A**.

Walk across the centre of the ensuing field, heading for another stile which soon comes into view. A brief crossing of the next field leads to an enclosed path. Follow this right, rounding buildings and into woodland.

When the path forks, branch left along the woodland boundary to enter Ipsden Wood, through which a clear path leads on to intercept another path at right angles (near a red-brick house).

PUBLIC TRANSPORT Buses to Stoke Row
REFRESHMENTS Pub in Stoke Row
PUBLIC TOILETS None on route
ORDNANCE SURVEY MAPS Explorer 171 (Chilterns Hills West), Landranger 175 (Reading, Windsor and surrounding area)

Maharajah's Well, Stoke Row

B Turn left onto a woodland path known as the Judges Road, and follow this (muddily in places) until it emerges at a surfaced lane (Busgrove Lane).

Busgrove Lane leads back to Stoke Row: turn left and follow it for 270 yards (245m) and then leave it for a rough track **C** on the right (Neal's Lane). The track climbs gently along the edge of woodland, and later becomes surfaced.

When Neal's Lane meets a track junction, turn left onto a sign-posted bridleway, that leads into Busgrove Wood, a mainly beech woodland. Just before the track reaches a road, keep an eye open for a footpath waymark on the left, pointing a way through the woods.

The path is clear, occasionally waymarked, and leads out to a lane.

Cross the lane onto a path opposite, to the right of a house. The path finally emerges onto School Lane. Turn right and retrace the outward route. ●

> **?** *How many 'portholes' can you count at the top of the Maharajah's Well?*

Cottisford and Tusmore Park

START Cottisford
DISTANCE 3½ miles (5.6km)
TIME 2 hours
PARKING Limited roadside parking near church
ROUTE FEATURES Farmland tracks, woodland, estate parkland

The countryside around Cottisford is forever associated with the 19th-century writer Flora Thompson (1876–1947), who brought the area to prominence in her novels of rural life in Lark Rise to Candleford. *Here you will find peaceful walking amid woodlands and across farm fields, reaching westwards to the great park of Tusmore House.*

Begin near the church in Cottisford, dedicated to St Mary the Virgin, and walk along the road to the turning for College Farm.

The church is a lovely example of Early English architecture consisting simply of a chancel, nave and south porch. In spite of alterations in 1861, the church retains much of the aura that would have prevailed in earlier centuries, a peaceful retreat in a tranquil corner of Oxfordshire.

Turn in at College Farm, following a broad, sand-coloured track. Beyond the farm, the track is flanked by high hedgerows

Millennium sundial, St Mary's Church, Cottisford

PUBLIC TRANSPORT None of any use
REFRESHMENTS None
PUBLIC TOILETS None on route
ORDNANCE SURVEY MAPS Explorer 191 (Banbury, Bicester & Chipping Norton), Landranger 152 (Northampton and Milton Keynes)

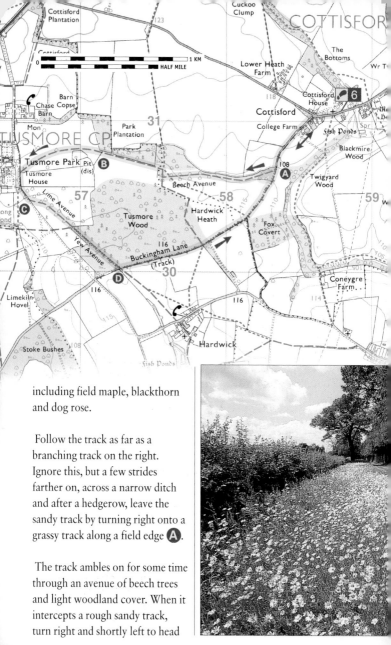

including field maple, blackthorn and dog rose.

Follow the track as far as a branching track on the right. Ignore this, but a few strides farther on, across a narrow ditch and after a hedgerow, leave the sandy track by turning right onto a grassy track along a field edge **A**.

The track ambles on for some time through an avenue of beech trees and light woodland cover. When it intercepts a rough sandy track, turn right and shortly left to head for the open parkland around Tusmore House.

At a fence and gate the on-going track enters estate parkland **B** and soon disappears. By continuing in roughly the same direction, however, a gate giving onto another estate track is finally

Trackside daisies, Tusmore Park

reached, not far from Tusmore House.

Turn left along the track, passing Tusmore House, and as a concrete driveway leads on, look for a gate on the left (blue waymark) giving once more into parkland **C**.

Through the gate go forward a short distance to walk down an avenue of lime trees. Follow the avenue to a gate beyond which the trees, now part of Tusmore Wood, are mainly yew and the track rather more overgrown.

Continue to the far side of Tusmore Wood and there intercept another track/path (Buckingham Lane). **D** Turn left onto a narrow path flanked by hedgerows and understorey.

The track runs along at the edge of woodland and finally emerges onto another sand-coloured estate track. Go forward along this and eventually rejoin the outward route, which can be followed back to College Farm and the church. ●

> **?** *Tusmore Park contains many fine examples of trees. See how many different species you can spot.*

7 The Thames and Oxford Canal

START	Port Meadow, Oxford
DISTANCE	3 ¾miles (6km)
TIME	2 hours
PARKING	Port Meadow
ROUTE FEATURES	Riverside paths, canal towpaths, city centre streets

This walk offers the chance of a break part way round to explore the stunning city centre architecture of Oxford or to find refreshment. The walk begins along a stretch of the Thames Path and returns between the Thames and the Oxford Canal. Keep an eye open for kingfishers.

Leave the car park and turn left towards gates giving into Port Meadow, and follow a clear path across to the River Thames.

Port Meadow, and the adjacent Wolvercote Common, is a large area of open grassland given to Oxford by William the Conqueror. It is mentioned in the Domesday Book, making it one of Oxford's oldest 'monuments'. It has never been ploughed or built upon, and is simply grazed by cattle and ponies. In winter, whenever the Thames floods, the meadow is host to flocks of ducks and geese. Horse racing was a big summer event on the meadow from 1680 to 1872, a tradition that was revived in 1980. These Oxford Races take place every July on Wolvercote Common.

Cross a wide, wooden bridge and, on the other side, double back left to follow the Thames Path, a lovely experience enlivened by waterfowl and river flowers, especially water lilies.

When the Thames Path reaches the Oxford Canal **A**, turn right over an arched metal footbridge, continuing beside the Thames, now behind terraced houses.

The Thames Path leads up to the A420 at Osney Bridge. Turn right, crossing the river, and, on the other side, cross the road with care (pedestrian crossing close by) to rejoin the Thames Path.

PUBLIC TRANSPORT Bus and rail services to Oxford
REFRESHMENTS Oxford
PUBLIC TOILETS Oxford
ORDNANCE SURVEY MAPS Explorer 180 (Oxford, Witney & Woodstock), Landranger 164 (Oxford & surrounding area)

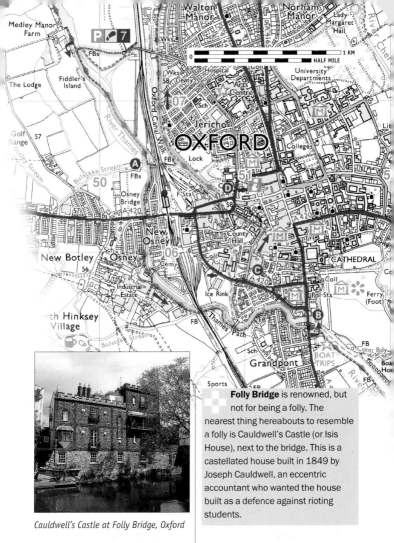

A — B — C — D markers shown on the map of Oxford, with features including Medley Manor Farm, Fiddler's Island, The Lodge, Golf Range, Osney Bridge A420, New Botley, New Osney, Osney, North Hinksey Village, Grandpont, Jericho, OXFORD, University Departments, Colleges, County Hall, CATHEDRAL, Ice Rink, Ferry (Foot), BOAT TRIPS, Thames Path, River Thames, Oxford Canal Walk, Bulstake Stream, Botley Stream.

0 — 1 KM
HALF MILE

Cauldwell's Castle at Folly Bridge, Oxford

Folly Bridge is renowned, but not for being a folly. The nearest thing hereabouts to resemble a folly is Cauldwell's Castle (or Isis House), next to the bridge. This is a castellated house built in 1849 by Joseph Cauldwell, an eccentric accountant who wanted the house built as a defence against rioting students.

Continue with the riverside path to reach Osney Lock, going past a weir and then press on beside the river to Folly Bridge **B**. Leave the Thames here by turning left over the bridge.

Turn into Thames Street and follow this to a major junction, crossing it at traffic lights. On the other side, go left towards the Duke of York pub, but turn right before then into Norfolk Street **C**.

The Thames, Port Meadow, Oxford

Norfolk Street later becomes Castle Street. At the far end, turn left into New Road. (*Anyone wanting to visit the centre of Oxford should leave the route at this point and turn right towards the city centre.*)

Continue past County Hall and go down to the end of New Road. Go left, crossing the end of Tidmarsh Lane and immediately cross the main road with care to reach a paved walkway (Fisher Row) beside the Oxford Canal.

At the end of Fisher Row, turn right over a road bridge, cross the road (a pedestrian crossing is nearby) and go onto a path alongside the Oxford Canal **D**.

Soon the path crosses a bridge at a lock, and then continues as the Oxford Canal Walk, passing the

The Oxford Canal on this side of the city was built between 1769 and 1790 to provide an outlet for Midlands industry, particularly coal. In 1796, the canal was linked to the Thames in Oxford by Isis Lock which was built by prisoners from the Castle Gaol.

Castlemill Boatyard, with the Thames on the left and the canal on the right.

Continue along the canal as far as a large factory, and there leave the towpath by ascending left at a bridge to reach a lane (Rutherway). Here take the first left and follow the lane down the road to return to the start.   ●

Find a milepost that isn't where it should be, and discover how far it is to Chipping Norton.

Badbury Hill and Great Coxwell

START Badbury Hill
DISTANCE 3½ miles (5.8km)
TIME 1½–2 hours
PARKING Roadside parking in Shrewsbury Lane
ROUTE FEATURES Woodland, farmland, country lanes

First visiting Badbury Hill, site of an Iron Age hillfort, this lovely walk combines woodland and farmland setting before trekking across country to the charming village of Great Coxwell, best known for its massive tithe-barn.

Walk through the car park, cross a step-stile, then go down through woodland. The path passes agreeably through the woodland, generally descending all the time. Ignore all branching paths, to come down to a broad woodland trail. Cross this, still descending, but now on a narrow path that leads out of the woodland and into the corner of an arable field.

St Giles' Church, Great Coxwell

Badbury Hill, cloaked largely by stands of beech and sycamore, conceals the earthen ramparts and ditch of an Iron Age defended settlement, roughly oval in shape and enclosing round huts, storage pits and pens for livestock.

A Go forward along the right-hand edge of an arable field heading towards Brimstone Farm, and, at the bottom of the field, bear left to a waymarked concrete

PUBLIC TRANSPORT Buses to Faringdon/B4019
REFRESHMENTS Faringdon, pub in Coleshill
PUBLIC TOILETS None on route
ORDNANCE SURVEY MAPS Explorer 170 (Abingdon, Wantage & Vale of White Horse), Landranger 174 (Newbury, Wantage and surrounding area)

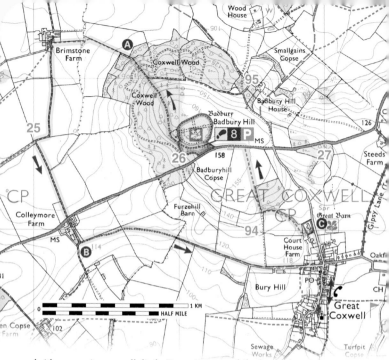

bridge spanning a small ditch. From this, walk up towards the farm.

At the farm, turn left on a surfaced access and follow this out to meet a main road near Colleymore Farm. Cross the road and go into the lane opposite (a bridleway signposted to Great Coxwell), walking past the farm.

When the on-going track forks **B**, bear left on a broad track across open farmland. Away to the south lies White Horse Hill with its conspicuous incumbent galloping for all eternity across its green slopes.

For a while the track wanders across open meadows, and then becomes enclosed between well-established hazel hedgerows.

The track becomes a lane at the

A short diversion to visit the **church of St Giles** is a good way of seeing Great Coxwell. The church itself is a delightful Norman structure, older than the nearby tithe-barn, and built on the site of a Saxon church of which nothing now remains except an entry in the Domesday Book. The churchyard is a lovely montage of relaxing headstones and wild flowers throughout most of the year.

edge of Great Coxwell, and continues forward as Puddleduck Lane, finally reaching the main village street.

Go left up the village street as far as a signposted turning at Great Coxwell Barn **C**.

Walk past the barn, keeping to the

Great Coxwell Barn is a magnificent structure. Thought by William Morris to be 'As noble as a cathedral', this is one of the largest tithe-barns in Britain, measuring more than 150 feet (45m) long and up to 50 feet (15m) high. The barn was built around 1250 after King John had granted the Manor of Faringdon to Beaulieu Abbey, a Cistercian monastery. The barn is now in the care of the National Trust.

right of a pond, to a waymarked gap giving into a large field. Turn right and walk around the field boundary.

The path runs up along woodland and then, at a stile, enters it briefly before leaving it to follow its boundary northwards towards Badbury Hill.

The path finally leads up to meet the main road. Turn left and walk the short distance back to the car park at Badbury Hill.

The farmland around Badbury Hill and Great Coxwell is much-favoured both by hares and partridge. See if you can spot either of these.

Great Coxwell Barn

9 *Letcombe Castle*

START Letcombe Regis
DISTANCE 3½ miles (5.8km)
APPROXIMATE TIME 1½-2 hours
PARKING Limited roadside parking in Letcombe Regis
ROUTE FEATURES Downland trails, one long ascent, stiles, woodland

The two Letcombe villages, Regis and Bassett, are the nucleus of a strong horse-racing fraternity. They nestle among the folds of downland north of the ancient Ridgeway and are a lovely blend of old, thatched cottages and red-brick buildings. This walk from Letcombe Regis heads up onto the downs to reach the Ridgeway and Segsbury Camp before returning easily.

Begin from the church and turn along the lane signposted to The Ridgeway and Segsbury Camp. Follow this past rows of attractive cottages as it bends right and left.

At the next bend to the left, leave the lane by turning onto a signposted bridleway on the right. The track is flanked by chestnut, hazel, hawthorn and birch and

Letcombe Regis was a Royal manor of the Kings of Wessex and England, which explains the 'regis' suffix. It is a quiet and very attractive village of cottages and red-brick houses, and home to a number of successful racehorse stables.

Foxgloves

PUBLIC TRANSPORT Buses to Wantage
REFRESHMENTS Letcombe Regis (pub) and Wantage
PUBLIC TOILETS None on route
ORDNANCE SURVEY MAPS Explorers 170 (Abingdon, Wantage & Vale of White Horse), Landranger 174 (Newbury, Wantage and surrounding area)

provides ideal cover for a host of summertime birds.

When the bridleway is joined by a footpath near a gate, bear left and walk towards a metal gate (ignore a branching path on the right).

Cross a step-stile and go forward along a field edge, the on-going track climbs gently with Letcombe Bassett soon coming into view. Continue past the gallop and cross another stile and go forward along an enclosed path.

Go as far as a gate and stile on the right **A**. Over the stile, bear left on a grassy path towards woodland, entered at a waymarked stile.

A clear path leads through the woodland. On the other side, turn immediately left, descending briefly before beginning a long and steady uphill section, crossing a narrow pasture before emerging into ridge-top grassland.

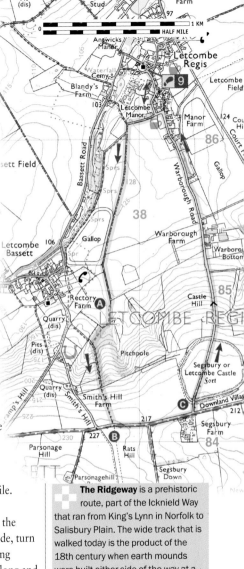

The Ridgeway is a prehistoric route, part of the Icknield Way that ran from King's Lynn in Norfolk to Salisbury Plain. The wide track that is walked today is the product of the 18th century when earth mounds were built either side of the way at a distance of 1 chain (28.11m) to protect the track from encroachment by ploughing.

From a stile, go straight across the ridge-top pasture to intercept the Ridgeway Path.

B Turn left along the Ridgeway which is flanked by some attractive and mature hawthorns, and continue for 600 yards (546m) to the turning on the left for Segsbury Camp **C**.

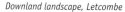 **Segsbury Camp** is a large (26 acres) Iron Age fort surrounded by a single ditch and embankment. Nothing remains within the site other than an air of mystery, though it is being managed to encourage the regeneration of grasses and wild flowers.

Leave the Ridgeway and head through Segsbury Camp, following a broad track which later becomes a surfaced lane and leads unerringly back down to Letcombe Regis.

On reaching the edge of Letcombe Regis, follow the lane briefly left, rejoining the outward route, and then right to work a way round to the church.

? *See if you can spot what date is associated with the letters T S.*

Downland landscape, Letcombe

Wayland's Smithy and Ashbury

10

START Ashbury Hill

DISTANCE 3½ miles (5.5km)

TIME 2 hours

PARKING Ashbury Hill

ROUTE FEATURES Chalk tracks, field paths, village lanes

Wayland's Smithy certainly has its place in history, but the village of Ashbury is not without its charms, among which are an attractive duck pond and 12th-century church. The walk is generally on good paths and tracks, but some of the paths are seasonally overgrown.

From the car park walk away from the road, following the Ridgeway Path for just over half a mile (1km) to a track junction. The main route turns left here. *Continue forward along the Ridgeway Path for another 300 yards (273m) to visit Wayland's Smithy* **A**, *set beside the Path in a shelter of trees.*

Return from the Smithy to the track junction and there turn right on a wide track flanked by mature hedgerows of hawthorn, blackthorn and field maple.

After about 500 yards (455m), just before a small area of woodland on

Wayland's Smithy is a large neolithic (Stone Age) burial mound, dating back around 5,500 years. Wayland is a mythical blacksmith, the son of a sailor hero and a mermaid, who later married a Valkyrie and eventually went to live with the immortals, making armour for the gods. The legend of Wayland's Smithy describes the belief that if a traveller's horse had lost a shoe, he had only to bring it to this place and leave the horse and some money. Upon his return, the money would be gone and the horse shod.

the right, branch left onto an indistinct narrow path descending beside the main track. A short way down this, keep an eye open for a step-stile (waymarked) over a fence on the left **B**.

PUBLIC TRANSPORT Buses to Ashbury (alternative start)

REFRESHMENTS Pub in Ashbury

PUBLIC TOILETS None on route

ORDNANCE SURVEY MAPS Explorer 170 (Abingdon, Wantage & Vale of White Horse), Landranger 174 (Newbury, Wantage and surrounding area)

Beyond the step-stile an elongated valley awaits, and, to its right, a thin strip of beech woodland reached by a vehicle track. The path, not always clear underfoot, lies along the base of the beech woodland and leads to another stile giving into an arable field.

Over the stile, keep forward along the base of a hill slope and at the edge of the field. After about 200 yards (183m) the path bears indistinctly to the right following a course around the end of the hill. The path **C** is seasonally overgrown (with nettles and cow parsley) and is not easy to spot (if you reach a fence you have gone too far and need only to backtrack a little to find the correct line). The path finally emerges at a step-stile giving onto a road at a junction.

Go forward along the road for Kingstone Winslow, following this as far as an abrupt left turn, and walk down to a village pond. Keep past the pond and walk up a gently rising bridleway (surfaced), which eventually emerges into Ashbury.

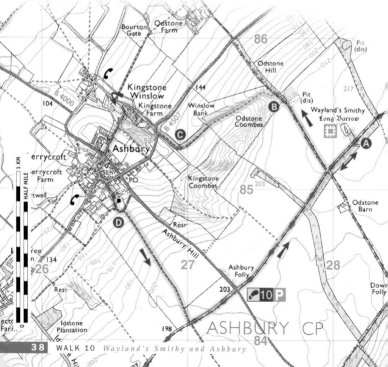

Wayland's Smithy

Cross into Chapel Lane, and follow the road through the village to another junction near the Rose and Crown Hotel.

Go forward, keeping to the right of the hotel, into Church Lane, and walk up to the church. Near the church (which is well worth a visit), bear right and immediately left onto a narrow pathway that leads up past the churchyard.

The path, gently rising, leads to an extension of the churchyard. As it bends right, go left onto another path. Shortly, when this starts to descend left, leave it by turning right onto a path **D** between arable fields rising steadily onto Ashbury Hill.

The Norman **St Mary's Church** dates from the 12th century, and is built on the site of a Saxon church. The church was probably cruciform in plan and had an aisleless nave. The church was enlarged in the 13th century, and the chancel rebuilt in the 14th. In the corner of the northern aisle is an unusual and interesting pre-Reformation fireplace – not the sort of thing usually found in a church.

The path finally emerges on the Ridgeway Path. Turn left, and follow the broad track of the Ridgeway back to the starting point of the walk.

See if you can find where I + W and I + N produces 1792.

11 *Cropredy and the Oxford Canal*

START Cropredy
DISTANCE 3½ miles (5.8k)
TIME 2 hours
PARKING Roadside, near Cropredy Bridge
ROUTE FEATURES Towpaths, farmland, roads

This is a gentle walk around the North Oxfordshire countryside, linking two villages of lovely cottages, each with interesting churches. Cropredy is the better known village, having been the site of a Civil War skirmish in 1644.

Start by crossing Cropredy Bridge and turning right, down

Oxford Canal, Cropredy

onto the towpath following the Oxford Canal away from the village.

During the English Civil War, once the Parliamentarian forces had gained possession of London, Charles I moved his court to Oxfordshire, but the war followed him there. In the churchyard at Cropredy are buried some of the forces engaged in the Battle of **Cropredy** Bridge (6 June 1644) when the king defeated the leader of the Cromwellian forces.

Leave the canal at Bridge 156 **A**: go under the bridge, climb up to a stile, and then double back over the bridge onto a broad track (Mill Lane) that passes Peewit Farm, a

PUBLIC TRANSPORT Buses to Cropredy and Great Bourton
REFRESHMENTS Pubs and Green Scene café in Cropredy, pub in Great Bourton
PUBLIC TOILETS None on route
ORDNANCE SURVEY MAPS Explorer 206 (Edge Hill & Fenny Compton), Landranger 151 (Stratford-upon-Avon, Warwick & Banbury)

railway crossing (take care here) and, finally rises gently to meet the Bourton road.

B Turn right to Great Bourton and, at Crow Lane (T-junction), go right again to the Cropredy road at another T-junction.

All Saints Church in Great Bourton is slightly off-route, but worth a detour. Originally, the church was 13th century, but was largely rebuilt in Victorian times. What is more interesting, however, is the eccentric Gothic lychgate, which features a tall openwork timber bell-tower with a steeply angled roof.

Walk alongside the road for 150 yards (136m) and then leave it by turning left through a hedge gap on a footpath signposted for Cropredy ⒸC. The path follows a field edge, and continues into a second field, where the field boundary changes direction. Keep forward to a footbridge giving into the next field, across which the path heads for the railway.

This time go beneath the railway line, and forward into the edge of Cropredy. At the village road, turn left, go past The Plantation into Station Road, pass the Brasenose Arms and then take the next turning on the right, at the village green. Go past the Green Scene café and turn right into Church Lane.

Enter the churchyard and turn left to a metal gate. Turn right to pass the Red Lion pub and walk down to reach the Oxford Canal. Cross the bridge, and turn left to return to the towpath, going left to the next bridge (153) and there go up steps to the Bridge Store.

Turn right over the bridge to return to the start. ●

> *How many canal bridges are met with on this walk, and can you spot any weather vanes?*

Mill Lane, Cropredy

Wroxton and Drayton

12

START	Wroxton
DISTANCE	3½ miles (5.6km)
TIME	2 hours
PARKING	Roadside, near duck pond
ROUTE FEATURES	Farmland, railway trackbed, woodland, parkland

North Oxfordshire is very much a farmland canvas onto which has been painted picturesque villages, many with a history, all with charm. This walk (seasonally affected by cropped-over fields) is a gentle wander through the countryside delighting in birdsong and wild flowers.

Begin from near the duck pond, complete with duck house and resident turtle as well as ducks, and take the lower road between Wroxton College and the pub, to reach the church.

Turn left past All Saints Church and walk up Church Street to the

Field path buried beneath poppies, Wroxton

Wroxton is a tranquil village of thatched, tawny brown marlstone cottages, built around the site of a 13th-century Augustinian Priory and a 14th-century church, although a church is recorded here in 1217, too. Many of the houses in Wroxton were rebuilt after a fire in 1666. Wroxton Abbey is today used as a university college.

PUBLIC TRANSPORT Buses to Wroxton and Drayton
REFRESHMENTS Pubs in Wroxton and Drayton
PUBLIC TOILETS None on route
ORDNANCE SURVEY MAPS Explorer 206 (Edge Hill & Fenny Compton), Landranger 151 (Stratford-upon-Avon, Warwick & Banbury)

St Peter's Church, Drayton

main road (Silver Street). Cross to the footpath opposite and follow the road ahead and then round to the right. After about 150 yards (136m), opposite a field gate on the other side of the road, turn left onto a signposted footpath **A**, striking out across an arable field.

Briefly enter woodland at Lord's Spinney and then continue up the next field to go through a hedge and, maintaining the same direction, eventually descend gently near a woodland.

The path now bears right from the field edge to enter the woodland, following a twisting route before swinging left to emerge at a road **B**.

Immediately turn right onto a hedged path that is the trackbed of a dismantled railway, and sports wild flowers and shrubbery typical of such a difficult habitat – hawthorn, dog rose, ash, oak, nettles and brambles.

Continue along the trackbed until a golf course and pond appear on the left, and then leave it by turning right through a hedge gap onto a bridleway **C** leading up to the edge of the village of Drayton which straddles the A422.

Go forward along a lane to meet the main road and there turn left, walking as far as the turning for St Peter's Church and here leave the road (signposted for North Newington). At a large building on the left (now a nursing home), cross a step-stile and walk down the ensuing paddock to another stile in the middle of a fence (to the left of a metal gate) **D**.

St Peter's Church, a little off-route but worth the detour, lies in a narrow valley nearby, and dates from Norman times. It is mainly built in the Decorated style, which dates from between 1290 and 1350.

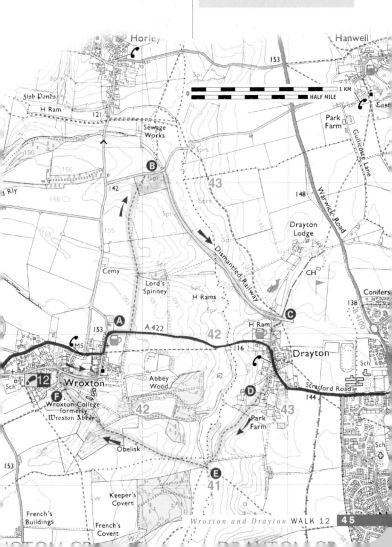

Cross the next field in the same direction, and in the one after that, pass an oak tree and a beech tree to locate another stile giving into a large arable field (seasonally overgrown with crops – the path, roughly parallel with a woodland boundary, is there, but you may have to fight your way through fields of poppies).

Finally, the path reaches a broad track **E**. Turn right through a woodland gap, cross a stone bridge spanning a stream, and go up the

See if you can pick out the sound of skylarks and yellowhammers.

ensuing pasture aiming for an obelisk on the skyline. The obelisk commemorates a visit of Frederick, Prince of Wales, in 1739.

Continue past the obelisk to a stile at the edge of the grounds of Wroxton College. Go down towards a lake and pass to its right to a gate. From the gate climb a grassy slope (no distinct path) to a metal gate and kissing-gate. Through the gate turn left to a strange polygonal structure **F**. This is a dovecote built in the ancient Gothic style by Sanderson Miller.

From the dovecote turn obliquely right and descend to a kissing-gate in the corner of the field. Beyond, an enclosed path leads out to Dark Lane. Turn right to return to the start.

The Obelisk, Wroxton

Great Tew

START	Great Tew
DISTANCE	3¾ miles (6.2km)
TIME	2 hours
PARKING	Great Tew
ROUTE FEATURES	Farmland, woodland

Great Tew is one of the most attractive villages in Oxfordshire: lovely ironstone, thatched dwellings flank a modest green and invite visitors into an other-worldliness that is the 17th century. From the village, this walk simply sets out to explore the surrounding countryside, making use of wide tracks and field paths.

Leave the car park at the edge of the village and turn left, going left again to walk down the village street, passing delightful thatched cottages before heading out into lightly wooded countryside.

Originally built for estate workers in the 1630s by Lord Falkland, the secluded village of **Great Tew** boasts perfect English cottages and a 17th-century, ivy-clad pub renowned for English Country wines and real cider, retaining much of its original period atmosphere. The village today is a fine example of landscape improvement set in a time warp. The cottage gardens with clipped box hedges were part of the 'landscape husbandry' pioneered by the youthful John Claudius Loudon in 1808 where, given complete freedom over matters of planning, his 'Theories of Beauty with Utility' took shape.

When the lane surfacing ends, continue left on a rough stony track as far as a track junction. Here, turn right on a path flanked by substantial chestnut trees, along with cedar and younger ash, sycamore, beech, oak, willow and hazel.

Continue as far as a branching track on the right, and here turn right along Groveash Lane **A**.

When the track escapes woodland it continues in the same direction along the edge of a field, flanked

PUBLIC TRANSPORT Buses to Great Tew
REFRESHMENTS Pub, Great Tew
PUBLIC TOILETS None on route
ORDNANCE SURVEY MAPS Explorer 191 (Banbury, Bicester & Chipping Norton), Landranger 164 (Oxford and surrounding area)

Great Tew

about 200 yards (183m) before a large staghead oak tree **B**, leave the main track and turn right across an arable field on the right-hand one of two possible tracks.

for a while by a hedgerow of blackthorn, dog rose, ash and oak.

As the hedgerow heads off in another direction, keep forward and, at a waymark signpost

On the far side of the field go through a neck of woodland and then keep on in the same direction on a continuing bridleway flanked by hedgerows, and seasonally overgrown.

At the end of the track, pass through a gate and turn left along a field edge. Continue into the next field and keep going towards a gate giving onto a road. Just before the gate, turn sharp right onto a footpath across an arable field **C**, targeting a radio mast in the distance.

Maintain much the same direction across five fields in all, the last with a hedgerow on the right-hand side. When the hedgerow ends, it does so at a track junction. Take the second on the right **D**, and walk alongside a drystone wall

that marks the boundary of Great Tew Park.

The wall serves as a sure guide back towards Great Tew. The path eventually goes through a gate and forward as a rough track, finally reaching the village beside the Falklands Arms. Turn right and walk back up to the car park. ●

The countryside around Great Tew is populated in spring and summer by a host of butterflies. See how many different species you can find.

The village shop, Great Tew

14 *Broughton and North Newington*

START	Broughton
DISTANCE	5 miles (8km)
TIME	2–3 hours
PARKING	Limited roadside parking on lane to Broughton Castle entrance
ROUTE FEATURES	Farmland, villages, some uphill

This lovely walk with expansive views across the Oxfordshire countryside links the villages of Broughton and North Newington, and finishes by visiting the grounds of Broughton Castle and its ancient church.

Opposite the entrance to the grounds of Broughton Castle take a footpath, signposted for North Newington, which strikes clearly across successive arable fields to meet a road.

Cross the road, and deal with one more field before emerging on the North Newington road near the entrance to Park Farm **A**.

Go into the entrance to the farm, but immediately leave the farm track by bearing slightly left across a pathless, undulating pasture aiming to the left of the farm buildings to locate a stile and enclosed path between houses.

The path emerges into a village street (Park Lane). Turn left and walk out to the main road not far from the Blinking Owl Country Inn.

Go as far as the Manor House and village pump, and there turn right onto a signposted track, climbing gently past a school playing field. At the end of the field, turn immediately right alongside a hedgerow **B**. [*The path here is often overgrown: if it is impassable, walk past an adjacent allotment site and then follow a field edge path to regain the original line.*]

Continue along the field edge path to a stile in a corner. Keep on in the

PUBLIC TRANSPORT Buses to Broughton and North Newington
REFRESHMENTS Pubs in Broughton and North Newington
PUBLIC TOILETS None on route
ORDNANCE SURVEY MAPS Explorer 191 (Banbury, Bicester & Chipping Norton), Landranger 151 (Stratford-upon-Avon, Warwick & Banbury)

same direction to a stile on the right giving onto a surfaced access lane. Cross this and a grassy area with chicken coops to another stile, and then strike downfield to the bottom left-hand corner.

Another stile gives onto a field edge path. Maintain the same direction along this, and in the next field corner, cross a concrete bridge, followed by a second a few strides farther on. Then go up the left-hand edge of the next field.

At the far side of the field the path goes into broadleaved woodland.

The hillside above Broughton Road is known as **The Bretch**, but it also has an association with a Giant's Cave from which a tunnel ran through to Broughton Castle and is said to have been used by Civil War conspirators.

Continue until completely clear of woodland on the right-hand side, just after which the path meets a cross track (yellow waymark).

C Take the first turning on the right which soon starts to follow the top edge of a field with woodland on the right, and lovely, distant views of Bloxham and its steepled church.

Follow the field edge path, which later bends left and, after a brief climb, descends to enter a thin strip of woodland. At the bottom of the woodland, go left along a field

The Manor House, North Newington

Village pump, North Newington

margin to locate a waymark on the right.

Turn down steps into a rough parking area. Ignore the first path on the right, and walk ahead to a blue waymark. Here, turn right to gain a narrow path going right. Follow this to reach Broughton Road by ascending wooden steps **D**.

Cross with care (the road is very busy) to the track opposite (signposted for the Salt Way, and shared with the National Cycle Network). Follow this stony track (probably an old packhorse route) taking time to study the lush hedgerow vegetation on either side, which in summer is popular with a wide range of butterflies including painted lady, tortoiseshell and speckled wood.

Continue as far as a waymark sign on the left, and here leave the main track by turning right over a footbridge and, in the ensuing field, bear half right towards a farm.

Cross to a stile and keep heading towards Crouch Farm, crossing its access then bearing left along a field edge, aiming for the steeple of Bloxham Church in the distance, to reach a metal gate in the far right-hand corner. A few strides beyond the gate, switch sides of the hedgerow and walk alongside the hedge to a field corner.

When the hedge changes direction, go through a wooden gate in the next field, and turn left, following the field margin out to meet a road.

Turn right and, taking care against approaching traffic, follow the road to Broughton. At the edge of the village, where the traffic is diverted right, keep forward.

At a main road junction (not far from the start), turn left past the Saye and Sele Arms pub to follow a roadside footpath.

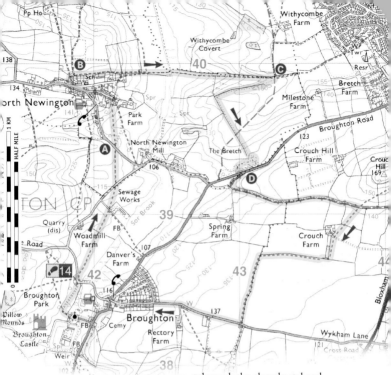

Broughton Castle was built on a moated site in the early 14th century as a fortified manor house rather than a castle. The house is historically significant, too, in that it was here that conspirators against Charles I met to plan their campaign, which soon led to the Civil War. The nearby Church of St Mary is of about the same age, thought to have been built around 1300. Broughton Castle is open from 18 May to 14 September, Wednesdays and Sundays, also Thursdays in July and August, Bank Holidays, Sundays and Mondays.

When the footpath ends, turn right on a paved path to the church. Go through the churchyard and emerge beside Broughton Castle. The grounds are open to walkers and, from the far side of the moat, you can get a good view of the castle even if it is closed. It was here that some of the filming for *Shakespeare in Love* and *The Madness of George III* took place.

Follow the estate road right to leave the grounds and return to the start. ●

> **?** *Who lived next door to the gardener?*

15 *Begbroke and Bladon*

START	Begbroke
DISTANCE	5 miles (8.2km)
TIME	2–2½ hours
PARKING	Roadside parking near Rising Sun pub
ROUTE FEATURES	Farmland, churchyard, stiles

This walk offers the opportunity to visit the Church of St Martin in Bladon, where Sir Winston Churchill, lies buried. It also calls in at St Michael's Church in Begbroke, a lovely Norman building set in a peaceful hamlet. The intervening farmland is a pleasure to wander, especially when summertime poppies sway in the breeze with the growing corn.

From the Royal Sun pub, turn down the lane signposted to St Michael's Church. The church lies off-route along St Michael's Lane, but is worth visiting. It is a small Norman church with a lovely south doorway arch. At the corner of St Michael's Lane, note the old Begbroke School House, now a private residence.

Follow the village lane to its end, and there turn right onto a bridleway (signposted for Bladon), initially setting off as a narrow path between hedgerow and wire fence.

From a gate go forward along a field edge eventually reaching the mixed woodland of Bladon Heath, entered at a gate **A**. The woodland is a cool and delightful place to be in summertime, when it rings loudly to birdsong.

On emerging from the woodland, keep forward along the right-hand edge of a narrow clearing flanked by extensions of the woodland. Shortly, reach the edge of a small housing estate at Bladon. Pass a row of garages and turn right (passing more garages) to a metal gate beyond which a lovely field-

PUBLIC TRANSPORT Buses to Begbroke and Bladon
REFRESHMENTS Pubs at Begbroke and Bladon
PUBLIC TOILETS None on route (except in pubs)
ORDNANCE SURVEY MAPS Explorer 180 (Oxford, Witney & Woodstock), Landranger 164 (Oxford & surrounding area)

Cottage, The Green, Bladon

edge path sweeps down to a path junction (signposted).

B Turn left here and follow the path towards Bladon. Shortly after the on-going path becomes a surfaced road, turn left into the graveyard of St Martin's church, and soon reach the Churchill family graves.

Bladon takes its name from the River Evenlode, which had the original name, Bladene. The village dates from Roman times, when it was settled in the third century. The early history of the village is involved with the quarrying of stone, used in many of the great buildings in Oxford. But Bladon is also renowned for its contribution to the local trade of glove-making, a Woodstock industry.

After visiting the Churchill graves and the church, walk out through the lychgate and go forward past The Green and along Church Street.

At the end of Church Street keep forward into Manor Road, and continue following the road until it bends sharply right (between houses numbered 35 and 37), and here leave the road by turning over a stile onto a path along a field edge.

When the hedgerow on the right ends, follow the path left to a step-stile on the right and an indistinct path running up the field edge to meet a road.

Go left along the road, taking care against approaching traffic, for about 200 yards (183m) and, just after Burleigh Lodge, take a step-stile (signposted to Yarnton) on the left **C**. Note the Millennium Stone here.

Follow a field edge path, and when the field boundary changes course, maintain the same direction, crossing the centre of an arable field. On the far side, cross a stile and then keep forward along the right-hand field edge. An overgrown stile gives access to the ensuing field, but there is an easier way through a gate gap.

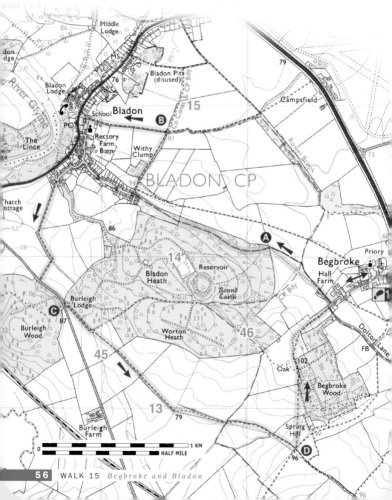

Across the next field, another stile gives into a large open pasture. Cross this, aiming for a hedge gap on the other side, beyond which a field edge vehicle track takes the

Keep following the field edge path to reach a gap in the hedge on the left (house in the distance), having just passed beneath overhead powerlines. This is Spring Hill.

From the gap **D**, strike obliquely left across the field to locate an overgrown stile in a low hedgerow, about 30 yards (27m) in from a

Stag horns are old trees which are dying and have already lost their uppermost canopy, so that the bare branches look like the antlers of a deer stag. See how many examples you can find.

broad track. From the stile, head up to another beside a metal gate and cattle grid. [*If the field is cropped over, the logic of following a legal right-of-way towards the house, then turning left on the broad track – not a right-of-way, but where usage seems to be allowed with the kind permission of the landowner – to rejoin the legal route at the cattle grid, will not escape notice.*]

Beyond the cattle grid, follow the continuing track which shortly swings right and descends to the edge of Begbroke, rejoining the outward route at the end of the surfaced lane, and retracing the outward route from there. ●

Grave of Sir Winston Churchill, Bladon

16 *Faringdon and Littleworth*

START Faringdon
DISTANCE 5 miles (8km)
TIME 2-2 ½ hours
PARKING Faringdon
ROUTE FEATURES Farmland, stiles

One of the objectives of this walk, Faringdon Folly, comes only at the end of the route after a long and peaceful trek across huge swathes of farmland between Faringdon and Littleworth. Although the busy A420 is never far away, there is a strong sense of isolation where you wander with no more than the sights and sounds of Nature.

In Faringdon walk up towards the church and turn right at the Faringdon Hotel. Ignore the turning to Witney. When the road bends right, leave it for a wide track to Church Path Farm (signposted to Thrupp).

Faringdon is an historic market town with a long and varied history of occupation by Prehistoric Man, Romans, Saxons, Normans and Vikings. The town was affected considerably during the Civil War (1643–1646), and so most of the buildings are of a later date, although largely unchanged over the past 200 years.

On reaching the farm, go through a gate on the left and along an

enclosed path, with fine views over the surrounding countryside.

At Grove Lodge **A**, keep forward, now walking along a field edge to reach Haremoor Farm. Here, cross two step-stiles either side of a farm track, and in the ensuing field bear obliquely left to a step-stile next to a

PUBLIC TRANSPORT Buses to Faringdon
REFRESHMENTS Faringdon
PUBLIC TOILETS Faringdon
ORDNANCE SURVEY MAPS Explorer 170 (Abingdon, Wantage & Vale of White Horse), Landranger 164 (Oxford and surrounding area)

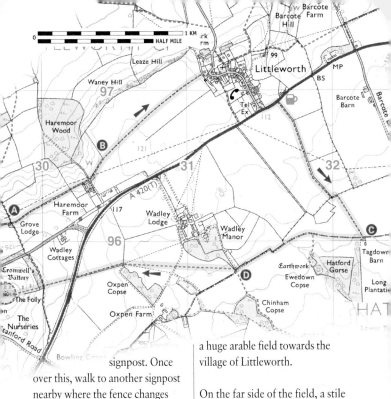

signpost. Once over this, walk to another signpost nearby where the fence changes direction **B**, and then strike across a huge arable field towards the village of Littleworth.

On the far side of the field, a stile gives onto a rough track leading, right, to meet the village lane. Turn right and follow the lane, past the church, eventually to meet the A420.

Turn left for 170 yards (155m) and, not far from the Snooty Fox Inn, cross the road with care and go along the

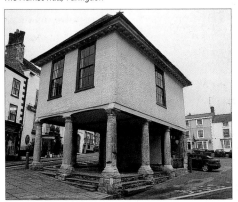

The Market Hall, Faringdon

signposted field track opposite. The track, seasonally overgrown, crosses between arable fields and then runs alongside a hedgerow. Stay with this when the hedge changes direction, but only a short distance farther on turn right to cross more fields, heading for Tagdown Barn **C** in the distance.

At the barn, turn right on a broad field track and keep following this for about half a mile (1km), finally leaving it at a white metal gate and stile **D**. Cross the stile and strike across another arable field, crossing an intermediate track, and on the far side of the field, at a second white gate and stile, continue out to meet the A420 once more.

The start of the on-going path lies over a step-stile a short distance to the left of a gate opposite, but the way is often overgrown and impenetrable. If this is the case, go through the gate and left along the field boundary to reach the stile, and from there head up the field to a white post.

From the post keep up the edge of the next field beyond which the path enters the circle of woodland surrounding Faringdon Folly. Continue past the folly, descending on a surfaced path that emerges on

Faringdon Folly

the edge of Faringdon at Standford Road. Turn right to a T-junction, and there go left to return to the centre of town ●

Faringdon Folly was built in 1935 by the 14th Lord Berners. It is the last major folly tower to be built in Britain, and was erected on the site of a medieval castle and Cromwellian Battery. The folly towers 100 feet (30m) and was originally colour-washed cream. The folly is open on the first Sunday in each month between April and October.

Staddle stones are small mushroom shaped pedestals originally used to keep small grain barns above the ground (and beyond the reach of rats). See how many you can spot on this walk; most are now used as garden ornaments.

Lower Heyford and Steeple Aston

17

This is a delightful amble through the Cherwell Valley, also making use of the Oxford Canal before heading cross-country for the attractive village of Steeple Aston. With a canal and river in such close proximity, this is a good place to spot a darting kingfisher.

START Lower Heyford
DISTANCE 5¼ miles (8.4km)
TIME 3 hours
PARKING Limited roadside parking in Market Square
ROUTE FEATURES Canal towpath, farmland, village streets, woodland, some uphill

Begin from Market Square by turning left at the Bell pub into Freehold Street. Go past the Old Bakery and the Old Bakehouse and then turn left into Mill Lane.

At the Oxford Canal, turn right along the towpath, closely paralleled by the River Cherwell.

Go past Allen's Lock at Upper Heyford, and soon leave the

The earliest recorded settlement at **Heyford**, close to a fording point of the River Cherwell, was in the 7th century. After the building of the Long Bridge in 1255 bringing increased trade and traffic, regular markets and fairs were held in Heyford until the 19th century. The Church of St Mary the Virgin is by far the oldest building in Lower Heywood, first consecrated in 1057. The earliest work in the present church, however, dates from the 13th century.

towpath at Bridge 203, turning left over a bridge spanning the Cherwell to enter a large field.

A Bear right to a concrete bridge across a stream, and then turn right, parallel with the stream, heading for a tunnel beneath a railway. From the tunnel head out on a narrow path into the ensuing field which gradually leads to a waymarked bridge at the edge of woodland.

PUBLIC TRANSPORT Buses and trains to Lower Heyford
REFRESHMENTS Pubs in Lower Heyford and Steeple Aston
PUBLIC TOILETS None on route
ORDNANCE SURVEY MAPS Explorer 191 (Banbury, Bicester & Chipping Norton), Landranger 164 (Oxford and surrounding area)

Cross the bridge and climb through a neck of woodland to reach and cross an arable field. At the top of the field, go through a wide hedgerow to access another field, and then turn right along a woodland boundary

> In the field above Steeple Aston is a strange structure, rather like the gable of a ruined barn. This is an 18th-century folly, the **Rousham Eyecatcher**, built by William Kent as a triumphal arch celebrating the victories in Spain of General Sir James Dormer of Rousham House.

Follow the field edge path to a gate giving onto a farm track **B**. Turn right, ascending gently towards the village of Steeple Aston. Go past cottages along Cow Lane to a T-junction near the church. Cross to the church, bearing left into North Street.

Walk along the road past the church and the old School House, and just before Tchure Cottage leave the road by turning onto a waymarked path between ironstone walls **C**.

> **Steeple Aston** is attractively situated on the north and south side of a small valley. Its church, dedicated to St Peter dates from the 13th century, with remodelling in the 14th and 15th century. The schoolhouse in North Street was founded in 1640 by the principal of Brasenose College in Oxford. Next door are two attractive almshouses with a sundial recording an 1814 rebuilding of the houses.

The path leads to a metal kissing-

Farmland landscape, Steeple Aston

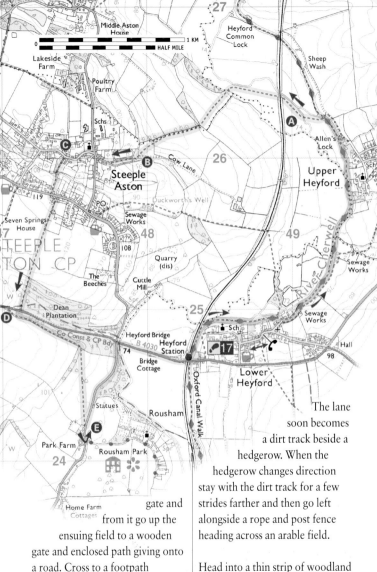

The lane soon becomes a dirt track beside a hedgerow. When the hedgerow changes direction stay with the dirt track for a few strides farther and then go left alongside a rope and post fence heading across an arable field.

Head into a thin strip of woodland on a path that leads to a stile, and in the ensuing pasture keep as much as possible to the left-hand edge to locate a stile and gate in the

gate and from it go up the ensuing field to a wooden gate and enclosed path giving onto a road. Cross to a footpath opposite (signposted for Rousham), which immediately bends left to meet a narrow surfaced lane, and there turn right.

The Oxford Canal, Lower Heywood

trees in its centre, and then aim to the right of a fenced pond. From the pond, head across to a large dead tree, and from there aim for a metal gate in the far corner, near Park Farm **E**.

Through the gate, turn left and walk beside the road, passing the grounds of Rousham House on the right, to reach Heyford Bridge. At this road junction, turn right towards Heyford, go past the railway station, and, just at the first houses on the left, turn sharp left to go down to the canal towpath.

far left corner, giving onto a busy road **D**.

Cross the road and go up a steep path opposite. At the top of the brief climb, turn left along a path flanked by mature chestnut trees at the top edge of a woodland boundary.

From a stile at the end of the woodland edge path, cross the next field by heading for two large lime

Bear right along the towpath, following the canal as far as the bridge used at the start of the walk. Turn back over the bridge and retrace the outward route up Mill Lane and along Freehold Street to the Bell Inn. ●

See how many crocodiles you can find on this walk.

Buscot and Kelmscott

START	Buscot
DISTANCE	5¼ miles (8.5km)
TIME	2½–3 hours
PARKING	Buscot
ROUTE FEATURES	Riverside path, roads, farm fields, country lane

18

Buscot and Kelmscott are two lovely villages, very much with the Cotswolds air about them. Both adjoin the River Thames and are linked in this walk by road and field walking. Kelmscott is renowned as the place where William Morris lived, and his house, Kelmscott Manor, is well worth a visit.

From the visitors' car park turn right and follow the surfaced track towards Buscot Weir. On approaching the weir, turn onto a narrow path leading to Lock Cottage and then cross lock gates and weirs to reach the Thames Path on the far side of the river. Here, the route crosses the county boundary into Gloucestershire, but will be back in Oxfordshire shortly.

Follow the Thames-side path, a very curvaceous experience as the river is in meandering mood. Keep an eye open in early June for the darting flight of demoiselle damselflies which feed on the

Buscot is a charming village of limestone cottages owned by the National Trust. Immediately on turning into the village visitors are welcomed by a substantial village hall and the unusual four-gabled shelter of the village pump, a product of rebuilding by the first Lord Faringdon in the late 19th century.

riparian greenery. The path courts the river faithfully and is flanked by an electrified fence.

As the path approaches an arched bridge **Ⓐ**, leave the riverside path by branching right through metal gate and along a broad track to meet a road.

PUBLIC TRANSPORT Buses to Buscot
REFRESHMENTS Tea Room in Buscot, pub in Kelmscott, restaurant at Kelmscott Manor
PUBLIC TOILETS Buscot
ORDNANCE SURVEY MAPS Explorer 170 Abingdon, Wantage & Vale of White Horse, Landranger 163 Cheltenham and Cirencester

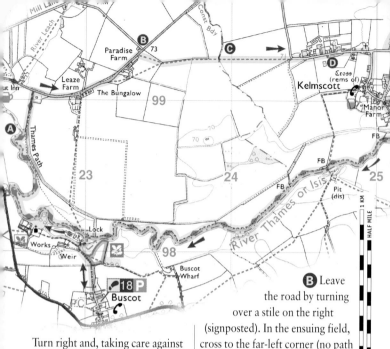

Turn right and, taking care against approaching traffic, follow the road for 800 yards (728m) until just past Paradise Farm.

Buscot village pump

B Leave the road by turning over a stile on the right (signposted). In the ensuing field, cross to the far-left corner (no path underfoot) and there cross a stile and bear left along a field boundary flanked by a high hawthorn hedgerow.

A stile in the next corner gives into a large arable field. Keep along the left-hand edge of the field, and when this sharply changes direction, keep ahead to locate a footbridge spanning a narrow stream across which the route returns to Oxfordshire **C**.

The large open fields hereabouts are favoured by hares, and it is not unusual to spot two or three hugging the ground or racing away.

Ahead lies a large arable field. The way across, usually trodden, roughly aims for a single tall, slim poplar tree among a group of trees in the distance. On the far side of the field, go forward onto a road that leads towards the straggling village of Kelmscott. [*Note: If the field is cropped over, you may find it easier to divert right, alongside the stream, to intercept a field track. Turn left along this.*]

Along the road, keep an eye open for a lovely carved relief of William Morris on some cottages **D** built in 1902 by Jane Morris to the memory of her husband. Opposite the church and next to the Old School, turn right, as if heading to the Plough Inn. Go past the inn, noting the base of an old preaching cross, and follow the road to the left.

As the road forks, bear right towards Kelmscott Manor. Note the interesting use of slabs of stone to form a field boundary alongside the road.

Continue past Kelmscott Manor and onto a signposted footpath for Radcot Bridge. Before long, however, as the track reaches the Thames, turn right over a small footbridge and through a gate to

Kelmscott Manor was the country home, from 1871 until his death in 1896, of William Morris, poet, craftsman, socialist and founder of the Arts and Crafts Movement. The house contains a fascinating collection of the possessions and works of Morris and his associates. (The Manor is open to the public from early April until the end of September but only to a limited extent. Telephone 01367 252486 for information.)

gain a grassy path along the northern bank of the river (signposted to Lechlade).

Once again, enjoy the twisting trail of the Thames as the path steadily heads back to Buscot. On the approach to Buscot Locks, cross a wide bridge and step left over a low stile following the path until it emerges at the edge of Buscot Locks.

Cross at the second lock gate and walk to the bridge spanning the weir, then head out past Lock Cottage to meet the lane leading left back to Buscot.

Can you discover two dates when the Thames reached abnormal heights?

19 *Wallingford*

This pleasant walk favours both banks of the River Thames, making use of the Thames Path and less well-used pathways. There is much happening on the river at all times of the year, and this serves as a prelude to an exploration of Wallingford itself and its castle.

START Benson
DISTANCE 5½ miles (9km)
TIME 3 hours
PARKING Roadside, St Helens Way, Benson
ROUTE FEATURES Riverside paths, roads, field paths and tracks

On the edge of Benson there is roadside parking along St Helens Way. Start along a

Church steeple, Wallingford

signposted footpath near The Cuckoo Pen Nursery, and head through an allotment site to a step-stile on the far side, beyond which a narrow paddock gives onto an A-road.

At the road turn left, walking to another path that emerges onto the road a short distance away. Cross the road with care, and go along an enclosed path opposite that finally emerges at a minor road. Turn right and walk as far as a signposted path (Thames Path: Wallingford) on the left.

Turn onto the path and follow it onto the weir spanning the Thames; it leads to Benson Lock

PUBLIC TRANSPORT Buses to Benson
REFRESHMENTS Pubs in Wallingford
PUBLIC TOILETS None on route
ORDNANCE SURVEY MAPS Explorer 171 (Chilterns Hills West, Henley-on-Thames & Wallingford), Landranger 175 (Reading, Windsor and surrounding area)

Wallingford Bridge

A, crossed by lock gates. On the other side, turn onto the Thames Path and follow this, faithfully hugging the river, all the way to Wallingford Bridge.

At Wallingford Bridge the riverside path is ushered briefly away from the river into Castle Lane and out to the High Street in Wallingford. Turn left and cross the bridge, on the other side going down steps and beneath the bridge to pursue a path on the opposite side.

Continue alongside the Thames, passing through two gates, and keeping forward after the second until roughly level with an isolated tree in mid-field, near a powerline pole: Newnham Farm stands not far away on the left.

B Leave the riverside path and turn abruptly across a field towards the tree and pole. There is no clear path on the ground (unless someone has walked before you). But on the other side, bear right towards the farm. Go through a metal kissing-gate and past farm buildings to locate a low step-stile on the left giving onto an access track.

Turn right onto the track and follow it out towards the A4130.

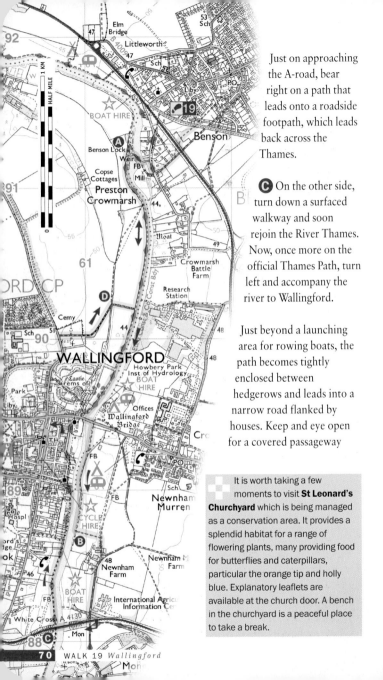

Just on approaching the A-road, bear right on a path that leads onto a roadside footpath, which leads back across the Thames.

C On the other side, turn down a surfaced walkway and soon rejoin the River Thames. Now, once more on the official Thames Path, turn left and accompany the river to Wallingford.

Just beyond a launching area for rowing boats, the path becomes tightly enclosed between hedgerows and leads into a narrow road flanked by houses. Keep and eye open for a covered passageway

It is worth taking a few moments to visit **St Leonard's Churchyard** which is being managed as a conservation area. It provides a splendid habitat for a range of flowering plants, many providing food for butterflies and caterpillars, particular the orange tip and holly blue. Explanatory leaflets are available at the church door. A bench in the churchyard is a peaceful place to take a break.

Benson Lock

and eventually emerging into a large pasture at a field gate and kissing-gate not far from the Thames **D**.

Walk along the field edge to rejoin the Thames Path, and turn left, now retracing the outward route.

through the houses that leads to the rear of St Leonard's Church. Have a look, too, for the marker on the wall of a house showing the water level on the Thames in November 1894.

From the church continue along Thames Street, and at its end turn left into High Street. Walk through Wallingford to reach Castle Street. Turn right here, and shortly take time to turn into Castle Gardens and explore the remains of Wallingford's Norman castle.

From Castle Gardens, continue along Castle Street, walking away from Wallingford. Follow the road until just past the entrance to a cemetery, and there take a signposted track on the right leading between cemetery grounds

At Benson Lock, cross the lock gates and weir and walk out to meet a back lane. Turn right for a short distance as far as a signposted path for Benson on the left. Follow the path to a major road. Cross with care and turn left for the short distance to the stile giving into a narrow paddock, beyond which lies the allotment site crossed at the start of the walk.

On the far side, turn into St Helens Way to complete the walk. ●

> **?** *Can you discover the name of the house where George Dunlop Leslie, a Victorian landscape painter, lived.*

20 Woodstock and Blenheim Great Park

START	Woodstock
DISTANCE	6½ miles (10.4km)
TIME	2½–3 hours
PARKING	Woodstock, Hensington Road car park
ROUTE FEATURES	Estate road and paths, woodland, farm fields

The opportunity to wander around the grounds of Blenheim Great Park is not one that should be missed. The route of this walk is easy to follow, and gives some delightful cameos of distant Blenheim Palace. The farmlands are populated with partridge, pheasant and rabbits. Woodstock itself is a lovely village in which to spend time.

Leave the car park and walk out to the road, turning right to the main road through Woodstock (A44). Turn right again and walk through the village alongside the A44, moving to the left-hand side at a pedestrian crossing and continuing out as far as a signposted bridleway on the left (just before the Black Prince pub) which turns through a large double gate with the number 95 on it **A**.

Go through another gate into Blenheim Park, and there bear right along a surfaced estate road, passing Queen Pool with a fine view of Blenheim Palace in the distance.

The ornate splendour of **Blenheim Palace** is the home of the 11th Duke of Marlborough and birthplace of Winston Churchill, Prime Minister of Britain during the war years. The palace was built as a national monument and not as a home. The Royal Manor of Woodstock and funds to build a palace were presented by Queen Anne to John Churchill, 1st Duke of Marlborough, as a token of the nation's gratitude for his successes in defeating the French army at Blenheim on the River Danube in 1704.

PUBLIC TRANSPORT Buses to Woodstock
REFRESHMENTS Woodstock
PUBLIC TOILETS At start
ORDNANCE SURVEY MAPS Explorer 180 (Oxford, Witney & Woodstock), Landranger 164 (Oxford & surrounding area)

In Blenheim Great Park

(1.2km) until, just before a cattle grid, it intercepts a lateral track, a Roman road (Akeman Street) (signposted for the Wychwood Way).

Ⓑ Turn left alongside a fence to a stile beside gates and continue initially beside woodland and then across a number of arable fields, crossing a farm track, and finally reaching the edge of a thin strip of woodland.

At a track junction near a cottage, bear right, continuing on an estate road that starts to climb gently and then bears left. As the ascent levels, the track bears right along a very wide drive flanked by double rows of small-leaved lime trees.

Now continue along the driveway for three-quarters of a mile

Enter the woodland and turn left on a rutted track, following this for about 200 yards (183m), and then branch left over a bridge to emerge at the edge of an arable field. Turn

The Grand Bridge, Blenheim

right, following the woodland boundary, and then strike across more fields to a line of pine trees in the distance.

C Bear left alongside the trees to rejoin the farm track, and turn right. Only a short distance on, abandon the track by crossing two stiles in quick succession (on the left). From the second stile strike out on a grassy path across a field roughly aiming for a fenced, circular stand of copper beech trees in mid-field.

Pass the trees and continue to another stile over a fence. Turn right and walk around the edge of another circular stand of copper beech (no path). Then follow a fenceline towards Park Farm.

At the farm edge, cross a step-stile and turn left on a surfaced estate road, passing round the farm and a line of well-established horse chestnut trees. Go left with the

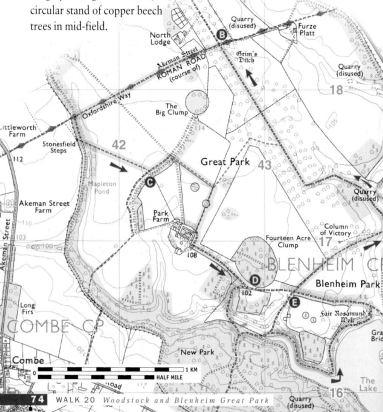

road, walking away from the farm and as far as a road junction on the right.

D Turn right, descending gently, the road flanked by mature beech trees, and, a short distance after crossing a cattle grid, leave the surfaced driveway by turning left (near a notice welcoming walkers to the park) onto a gently descending grassy path that leads to a gate near the western end of the park's main lake.

Through the gate, bear right, following the edge of the lake, which is dotted with water lilies, and keep following the lakeside path as it twists and turns to reach a gate near Grand Bridge. Now there are

some lovely views of Blenheim Palace in the distance.

From the gate, turn left onto a driveway, walking away from Grand Bridge, and continue as far as stiles spanning electrified fences either side of the drive. **E** Go right here, and soon stay parallel with a fenceline to reach the Column of Victory.

From the column, walk in the direction of the houses of Woodstock in the distance (no path), and then descend to locate another stile/electrified fence along the edge of a surfaced drive.

> With a lengthy inscription that explains its purpose, the **Column of Victory**, is a fluted Doric column surmounted by a statue of the Duke of Marlborough and Roman eagles.

F Once over this, go left and, at a cottage, bear right, rejoining the outward route, and following this back to the A44 and Woodstock. ●

> *Along many farmland walks you find a ground-hugging, plant with a bulbous yellow head which, when crushed gives off the scent of pineapple. See if you can find any.*

Further Information

Walking Safety

Although the reasonably gentle countryside that is the subject of this book offers no real dangers to walkers at any time of the year, it is still advisable to take sensible precautions and follow certain well-tried guidelines.

Always take with you both warm and waterproof clothing and sufficient food and drink. Wear suitable footwear, i.e. strong walking boots or shoes that give a good grip over stony ground, on slippery slopes and in muddy conditions. Try to obtain a local weather forecast and bear it in mind before you start. Do not be afraid to abandon your proposed

A well-maintained field path

route and return to your starting point in the event of a sudden and unexpected deterioration in the weather.

All the walks described in this book will be safe to do, given due care and respect, even during the winter. Indeed, a crisp, fine winter day often provides perfect walking conditions, with firm ground underfoot and a clarity of light unique to that time of the year.

The most difficult hazard likely to be encountered is mud, especially when walking along woodland and field paths, farm tracks and bridleways – the latter in particular can often get churned up by cyclists and horses. In summer, an additional difficulty may be narrow and overgrown paths, particularly along the edges of cultivated fields. Neither should constitute a major problem provided that the appropriate footwear is worn.

Follow the Country Code

- Enjoy the countryside and respect its life and work
- Guard against all risk of fire
- Take your litter home
- Fasten all gates

- Help to keep all water clean
- Keep your dogs under control
- Protect wildlife, plants and trees
- Keep to public paths across farmland
- Take special care on country roads
- Leave livestock, crops and machinery alone
- Make no unnecessary noise
- Use gates and stiles to cross fences, hedges and walls

    (The Countryside Agency)

Useful Organisations

Council for the Protection of Rural England

Warwick House, 25 Buckingham Palace Road, London SW1W 0PP. Tel: 020 7976 6433; Fax: 020 7976 6373; Email: cpre@gn.apc.org.

English Heritage

23 Savile Row, London W1X 1AB. Tel: 020 7973 3434; Fax: 020 7973 3001; Website: www.english-heritage.org.uk.

English Nature

Northminster House, Peterborough, Cambridgeshire PE1 1UA. Tel: 01733 455100; Fax: 01733 455103; Email: enquiries@english-nature.org.uk; Website:www.english-nature.org.uk.

Forest Enterprise (England)

340 Bristol Business Park, Coldharbour Lane, Bristol BS15 1AJ. Tel: 0117 906 6000; Fax: 0117 931 2859.

National Trust (Thames and Chilterns)

Hughenden Manor, High Wycombe, Buckinghamshire HP14 4LA. Tel: 01494 528051; Fax: 01494 463310.

Ordnance Survey

Romsey Road, Maybush, Southampton SO16 4GU. Tel: 02380 792912; Fax: (Public) 02380 792615; Email: custinfo@ordsvy.gov.uk; Website: www.ordsvy.gov.uk.

Ramblers' Association

2nd Floor, Camelford House, 87–90 Albert Embankment, London SE1 7TW. Tel: 020 7339 8585; Fax: 020 7339 8501; Website: www.ramblers.org.uk.

Royal Society for the Protection of Birds (RSPB)

The Lodge, Sandy, Beds SG19 2DL. Tel: 01767 680551; Fax: 01767 692365; Website: www.rspb.org.uk

Woodland Trust (England and Wales)

Autumn Park, Grantham, Lincolnshire NG31 6LL. Tel: 01476 581111; Fax: 01476 590808; Website: www.woodland-trust.org.uk.

Local Organisations

Southern Tourist Board
40 Chamberlayne Road, Eastleigh, Hampshire SO5 5JH. Tel: 023 8062 5500; Fax: 023 8061 8018; Email: info@southerntb.co.uk.

Oxford Information Centre
The Old School, Gloucester Green, Oxford OX1 2DA. Tel: 01865 726871.

Oxford Tourism Management
2nd Floor, St Aldate's Chambers, St Aldate's Oxford OX1 1DS. Tel: 01865 252172.

Oxfordshire County Council
Tel: 01865 810292.

South Oxfordshire District Council
Tel: 01491 823748.

West Oxfordshire District Council
Tel: 01993 770347.

Cherwell District Council
Tel: 01295 221725.

Local Tourist Information Centres

Abingdon: 01235 522711.
Banbury: 01295 259855
Bicester: 01869 369055
Burford: 01993 823558
Chipping Norton: 01608 644379.
Henley-on-Thames: 01491 578034
Thame: 01844 212834.
Wallingford: 01491 826972
Wantage: 01235 760176.
Witney: 01993 775802.
Woodstock: 01993 811038.

Public transport

Bus Traveline: 0870 608 2 608
National Rail Enquires: 08457 48 49 50
(www.thetrainline.com)

Ordnance survey maps of Oxfordshire

Explorer maps: 206 (Edge Hill & Ferry Compton), 191 (Banbury, Bicester & Chipping Norton), 180 (Oxford, Witney & Woodstock), 171 (Chiltern Hills West), and 170 (Abingdon, Wantage & Valle of White Horse).
Landranger maps: 175 (Reading, Windsor and surrounding area), 174 (Newbury, Wantage and surrounding area), 164 (Oxford and surrounding area), 163 (Cheltenham and Cirencester), 152 (Northampton and Milton Keynes)

Summer fields near Wayland's Smithy

and 151 (Stratford-upon-Avon, Warwick and Banbury.

Answers to questions

Walk 1: They are the numbers of the trig pillar on White Horse Hill.

Walk 2: The Danes. Part of the poem on the Poem Tree reads 'Around this hill the ruthless Danes intrenched'.

Walk 3: It would take a botanist to identify all the flowers encountered on this walk, but among them are cranesbill, vetch, dog rose, poppy and foxglove.

Walk 4: It was a grammar school in the 17th century.

Walk 5: There are 24.

Walk 6: Most of the trees were planted when the estate parkland was set out. Species, of which there are at least twenty, include horse chestnut, copper beech, Spanish chestnut, cedar, oak, elm, Scots pine, larch, ash and beech.

Walk 7: Beside County Hall is a milepost taken from the B4031. The distance to Chipping Norton is 8½ miles.

Walk 8: Partridge are a ground-hugging bird, and although they do fly when alarmed they prefer to run. Hares, by contrast, freeze, and try to blend in with their surroundings.

Walk 9: 1680. There is a date-stone on a thatched cottage near the start of the walk. More difficult to spot is the date 1707 and the letters I S E, set in flint into red brick on the gable of the cottage opposite the church.

Walk 10: These are the details on a date-stone set into the side of a cottage opposite the pond at

Kingstone Winslow, and probably represent the name of the people for whom the cottage was built.

Walk 11: Five bridges: 152–156. Weather vanes are a common feature on many farm buildings. There's one at Peewit Farm.

Walk 12: Skylarks are a reducing species in southern England, but abundant above the North Oxfordshire farmlands. Their unmistakable song is delivered on the wing. Yellowhammers have a distinctive call that sounds like the bird is asking for 'A-little-bit-of-bread-and-no-chee-eeeeese'.

Walk 13: The range of butterflies that frequent the Oxfordshire countryside is vast, but species that are easy to see include painted lady, peacock, small tortoiseshell, meadow brown and gatekeeper.

Walk 14: The wheelwright. In North Newington, just after the pub, are Gardeners Cottage and Wheelwrights Cottage.

Walk 15: The area around Bladon has a number of stag horn trees.

Walk 16: There are some in Littleworth both alongside the road and in gardens.

Walk 17: At the bottom of the garden at the rear of Tchure Cottage in Steeple Aston there is an ornamental display featuring three wooden crocodiles.

Walk 18: November 1894 and March 1947. Both flood levels are marked on a small building near the second weir at Buscot.

Walk 19: Riverside in Thames Street, near St Leonard's Church: information on doorway.

Walk 20: Pineapple weed, a member of the mayweed family.